Poetry Written out of Necessity

An Anthology

Featuring:

Penelope Lack
Sonia Nelson-Cole
Keith Clarke Holgate
Tricia Sturgeon
Christine Hornby
Ann F Bell

Edited by John Birch

Published by Spiritual Path Books UK
ISBN 978-0-9558832-3-1

Spiritual Path Books UK
Flat 4, 36-38 St Annes Road East, Lytham St Annes,
Lancashire FY8 1UR
Tel: 07887 500125

Contents

Preface

Poetry Written out of Necessity is an anthology of poetry taken from a small group of poets, each one bringing their own unique experiences, challenges and insights to this original, inspiring collection.

Each series of poems, truly written out of necessity, served originally to heal the writers themselves, but may now be offered up to others to help them heal also. The desire to heal others shows through in the works of each author.

From the traditional, yet mystical and philosophical style of Tricia Sturgeon to the classical, penetratingly spiritual depths of Penelope Lack's works (both to be published individually in 2009 by Spiritual Path Books UK); from the very simple, yet deeply experiential dialogue of Christine Hornby to the highly evolved, channelled wisdom and Truth of Sonia Nelson-Cole; from the posthumously published works of Keith Clarke Holgate – a man still very much in touch and proving the timeless healing of love – to the words that triumph over loss and pain penned by Ann F Bell; within these poems, every reader will find a corner where he or she may bathe in healing.

Enjoy the experience.

John Birch

Penelope Lack

Penelope feels that her poetry originates from her heart and soul. Much of it conveys a sense of loneliness, and the ways she finds solace, as well as joy, here in the physical plane.
During her Arts Degree in Chichester, Sussex (early 1990's) she was inspired by the simple and profound nature of Japanese Haiku poetry.
Born in the depths of winter (1952) she relates to the beauty of life pared down to the essential. A bleak place to be at times, yet she knows the cycle of seasons, and they all appear as she writes.
Her poetry is forever changing within these cycles, and in her individual, fuller collection (to be published by Spiritual Path Books UK in 2009) this is more visible, as her work becomes a living diary of her everyday life.
Returning from sleep or meditation, poetry becomes one of her reasons to live – a way to ease, as well as communicate, the anguish of separation from The Source. Her way is subtle, her heart softened by desolation, as well as impassioned to dance and sing.
At this time, she hopes people will feel relationship with her work, and as Divine Light pours down into the Earthly plane, creating a more sacred world for us all, she hopes they find inspiration too.
She thanks all those who have helped and supported her with their love.

Resplendent Midday Madness

Watching the blackberries stain
My summer blue dress.
The first woodsmoke rises;

Crushed lavender and white linen
Await your return.

And now the wood cracks and splits in the fire.
My skin grows soft
From the scented oils
You rub in each evening.

The frozen winter moon outside.

Once again, returning, climbing –
High amongst
The spring-supple leaves
Of the sycamore tree;

Alone. A zenith.

Surrendering to the heat,
Open pored,
I absorb

Resplendent midday madness.

The poppied corn and I –
Sparkling in our silence.

Softening

Spring storms and sunshine.
Yesterday – poetry everywhere I looked!
Today, pale grey sky.
Oh my heart is so lonely!
I arise and make evening soup.

Later, a short walk –
Dark grey clouds sharpen the sky.
There is scent of light rain
On tarmac and spring earth.
My heart is softening – slowly.

I Come to Rest
(Chichester Cathedral cloisters and the west door)

Today – wandering
Beneath blue sky and white clouds
And through the cool shadowy cloisters,
I come to rest beyond the heavy wooden doors –
The wind pushing at my back.
And I am reminded of yesterday
When I pushed at life
And all sense of peace escaped me.

Just to say…

A day of just doing
What needs to be done –
The washing,
Daily chores.

No joy inwardly –
No joy outwardly.
All feeling of love
Has disappeared.

It can be borne
By writing poetry.

Now I will go
And make supper
As my prayer to You.

That is all I can do,
And I am glad
That You know.

I Forgive

I sit in the quiet garden –
My neighbour's overhanging cherry tree
Still bare.

Any day now,
I will stand under the mass
Of delicate pink-flowering blossoms –
Open to this unearthly light.

And I will forgive everything.

The Monk's December Hut

The winter solstice
Pure
And white –
A crimson Christmas
Now in sight.

A bowl of tea
Fragrant
Black –
Is steaming
On the cotton mat.
Outside
Satin slippers
In the snow –
And silver bridesmaids
Barefoot go.

Stilled

It is a still day,
Misty and damp,
Dripping trees –
December.

There are two
Ring collared doves
In the cherry tree –
Side by side.

Just now –
One of their soft white underfeathers
Drifted down
Into the garden.

It has stilled me.

A Second Chance

Waking to the alarm this morning, she had covered her head with the duvet, and slept again.

The wind during the night had blown angrily, and she had woken numerous times – restless – feeling an intense anger rising in herself.

Getting up now, she was anxious to see if her landlord had left yet. She had not cared about missing his departure, when earlier she had so strongly felt the need for still and peaceful sleep – but now she thought she might still have the chance to say goodbye to him.

Carefully descending to his part of the house, she found his pannier packed and open – he had not yet left – only nipped out for a moment. She felt surprised by her relief, and a reassurance, offered as she was now – a second chance.

Returning, he was greeted by her rare smile of happiness at seeing him – surprising him, so that he looked at her carefully.

Sorting out a few household details, she then kissed him gently beside his mouth, in a well-wishing goodbye, and left him to his usual pre-holiday rush. Returning to her room, she heard the front door close soon after.

Breakfast, a letter written, a little reading and a simple lunch – now, finding her book hard work, she just sat, suddenly feeling the space left by the landlord's departure.

Late afternoon –
The winter's day,
With its strong wind and rain
Around the house
Was her companion now.

In that moment, she knew she would not fill the space with exhaustive activity. She would let the emptiness fill and still the house she was now to look after – and she would do so quietly – with whatever love she had.

This was her work, this was her loneliness. As she stirred herself to make some hot tea, tears filled her eyes – and in a surprisingly tender way, sheets of fine rain were thrown against the window glass.

I set you Free

There seems no point
To anything
After my long afternoon sleep.

But I am hungry
And the neighbour's boy
Is yelling with such gusto,
That I do return –
Gently.

Layered sheets of
Orange and fuchsia tissue paper
Catch the evening sunlight,

And my returning visions
Of sacred spaces, full
Of coloured light –
Ethereal, translucent,
Are with me
In all their
Great ambitiousness.

The horseradish bites –
The buttercake is sweet,
My appetite appeased.

I have made The Journey
Once again,
And now –
A rainbow
Of light
Comes through the window.

God's grace is with me.
And now I am longing
For love
In more human form,

And for Him to say –
I bless you.

I bless you
And I love you.

I know your pain
Your aching,
Your longing
And your desperation.

I know you must be
In this world
Without the love
Of those you love.
Without the love
Of those who loved you.

And I know how much you long
For a sweet love.

I see your anguished face,
Your torment.

I see your desolation.
And as I set you free
Into this world,
Grieve me for a while –
Then in your softness,
Love –
As I love you.

Lament

I eat –
Hot nourishing
Vegetable and chicken soup
From the old saucepan,
Dented from a furious
Rageful throwing
In the past.

The heat
Seeps
Into me –
Warming my autumn-chilled body.
My sneezing stops,
And I lament
My inability
To restore this house
To love.

Blessing

(Chichester Cathedral cloisters – western arm)

The beauty of the paintings
The gentle love in the artist –
We talk of silence,
And stillness.

Afterwards – amongst the lime trees,
I am refreshed by cold apple juice,
The clarity of light,
And autumn air.

To find a solitary
And quiet spot,
I wander through the cloisters.

Embraced by the stone alcove
I enjoy my picnic –
A shaft of afternoon sunlight
My companion.

Then – standing to stretch my legs,
I turn to find
I have been sitting under a blessing
Written on the wall
That talks of The Silence.

Being Mouse

What a cat! Mouse!
Just being himself,
Loved and loving.

For Sheena as Woman

It is a midwinter morning –
Alone and peaceful
I sit in my curtained kitchen.

The glass-backed candle
My friend has given me
Is alight.

I wonder at her patience,
And impatience
With me,

And I thank her
For remembering me.

Reborn from a darkness
To which the cycle
Will return me,
I see how we are like
The moon
With all her moods –

And we have not been recognised
Nor understood.

Today,
I have stopped fighting
And protesting
For I am too busy living
As woman.

My pale tea –
Delicate,
Strengthens and sustains
My whole,
As I gently go into this day.

Cloistered,
In this neglected home,
I think to how
I'll later light the fire
Above a stoneless hearth –

And ask,
That if I die
Before my poems
Should all be heard

That friends true,
With family faithful,
Will gather them
Into wholeness
For the world.

Simplicity

In this moment
I am happy.

The cream and blue tea cloth
Is warm from the radiator,
And able to dry my soup bowl.

In such a complex world
I hold to this simplicity.

African

And I watch the tall Sudanese woman –
Seeing the weight of her slender hands
As they bend backwards on her flexed wrists
Whilst she talks.

And as I eat and bathe,
My hands are hers
And hers mine.

She is easy in her body,
And when I crouch in the bath
Wiping the sides,
I am an agile African child –
Black-limbed and lithesome.

Hope

I awake from a brief, deep sleep –
Early evening,
And lay a while, quietly.

I summon up reason to move.

I recall the beauty of yesterday –
Cathedral gardens, fish pond
Green and dark.
Tranquillity in cool fresh air,
Crocuses luminous
In gentle rain.

This remembrance helps me arise,
Although the beauty
Was of yesterday.

I go about small tasks
And contemplate how past is always leaving,
Present slips away –
And hope arises in the coming moment.

I feel to keep these moments
Past present future, close together,
In the cycle of each breath –
Whole again.

Love Finds its Way

Out into the cool fresh air
Of the early spring dusk –
And gently,
From the brick and stone
Comes the warmth
Absorbed from the day's sunshine.

Aware of the scents and feelings
Where day and night meet –
And how I follow,
And go before
All my neighbours,
Our paths interweaving through time,
I realise
Love has found its way
Into this meeting place,
Where the new season
Is blessing everything
And everyone.

Of Remembrance

I place the unwashed teaspoon
From the golden marigold tea
On a plate.

If it leaves a stain there
I will be quite glad –

For it would remind me always
Of this moment –
A moment when nothing seems to matter anymore.

Simple Faith

Today I sit
In the space of a quiet moment –
Hot green tea from the white mug
Releasing all anxiety and doubt
From within.

Close by –
A white chrysanthemum with green leaves
To meditate on.

I rest awhile,
Feeling that kind of Faith and Trust
I have seen in others
Which brings an exquisite beauty
To their being.

Peace washes through you
When you know
That God is looking after you –
And all is well.

Thank You.

Love's Garden

Childhood summer,
Forever sunshine.

Mum and Dad
Brother and sister –
Ever present.

Long back garden,
Grass,
Small walls and rocks.
Fragrant peppery Pinks,
Dahlias full of earwigs!
Snow-on-the-Mountain – so soft.

Wasp stings,
Bounding Daddy-long-legs.
Swings,
Paddling pools.
Little model aeroplanes,
Boats.

How I wish I could go back now
And talk to us all then –
How I miss you all!

Containment

The fading month of August
Becomes contained
Within arrival of each evening's hues,
Within each sigh
And lengthened pause,
So gradual, yet we can't ignore
These moments, as our slowing steps
Begin to wend another spiral circle
From Beyond.

So little outward sign,
We cannot hurry time,
But I gently assume
My heart is asking me
To stop a while
And ponder Thee…

Resolved

The last of the cherry blossom
Is being blown from the tree.
Spring has filled the garden with greenness
Into which these tiny white petals fall.

I am dancing –
Enjoying the feeling of my bare arms
As they sweep through the air in circles.
I am so lonely, and have been for so long
That I wonder if I will ever not be.

Earlier, I crouched on the grass
Singing a little song about Jesus
That I made up as I went along,
In a kind of comforting joy
As you sing to a child in encouragement.

The day will end and I will sleep,
Tomorrow will come and my life will move on,
Alongside other people's –
So yes, I am part of life.

For now, I will wash the lettuce leaves
To eat alongside my baking supper,
Just doing one thing after another,
Feeling I have resolved nothing
Because I do not know how…

Sonia Nelson-Cole

Sonia Nelson-Cole has been writing poetry since the age of 14 when she came second in a poetry competition, which was part of 'The Eisteddfod', held in Warwickshire where she went to school. All of her work is inspired through personal experience and her observations of life, our world and of the universe. Over the years Sonia found writing helped bring understanding and healing into her life, which has led to considerable personal growth.

As others share their own experiences and thoughts, Sonia is intuitively aware of their inner feelings, and is thus inspired to write with the intent to convey an insight into these experiences.

Most of the poems featured here are from Sonia's unpublished book *A Fountain of Experience*, which is a compilation of many of her writings over the years.

Sonia has facilitated workshops and meetings, providing guidance to others on the use of writing to help them understand and grow from their lessons and experiences in life. She is working on producing inspirational cards, using her poems as the theme.

Although she spent her childhood and teenage years in England, she was born in Lagos, Nigeria, where she spent most of her adult life. She is married with four children and four grandchildren and now lives in London, working for a children's charity.

A Fountain of Experience

We immerse ourselves in the sea of Life:
The waters swirl around us
Sweeping us into the fathoms of the deep,
Swaying and twirling to the rhythms of the tides.

And in these depths
We hear the wailing and the cries
Of the suffering.
We see the torment and the anguish;
We feel the sadness and the sorrow,
In the depths of the darkness.
    And all these things lie within our being,
    For we experience these things.

And yet in these depths
We also hear the laughter and the joy
Of the beloved;
We see the beauty and the blessings
Of life.
We feel the love and the happiness
Which encompasses us.
    And all these things lie within our being,
    For we experience these things.

As we slowly rise up
From the depths,
We are immersed in the cleansing waters.
For we are filled
With such understanding
From these experiences:

And the knowledge gained
Brings Wisdom,
Light and Love;
Creating
A Fountain of Experience
Within us,
For all time.

Be Still My Soul

Be still my soul,
Be still;
Let not the waves of life
Toss you into the sea of emotion;
Let not the rising tides
Disrupt your tranquil mind.

Be still my soul,
Be still.

Quiet the mind,
Be still.

Let peace fill your soul;
Let the waves toss and turn,
But be still.

Be at peace
For the turmoil will cease,
And the sea calm.

So still,
Peace, peace, peace.

Memories Are For all Time
(Hold Your Memories In Your Heart)

All thru' our lives
We are gathering
Memories,
The bitter and the sweet together.
They are embedded in familiar buildings,
In possessions acquired,
In the people we meet along life's path;
In those we love.

But more important,
These memories
Are embedded in our hearts.

It is not in material things
Which gather dust and wither away;
Nor in the human form
Which dies and decays;
It is in the hearts and souls
Of humanity
That these memories lie
For all time.

So as we put away
Those physical reminders,
We can let go of the past;
For we hold the memories
Deep in our hearts.
And we can then look to the present
And be thankful for these memories,
For they are a reminder
Of all the blessings
We have received along the way.

The Dreamer's Dreamless Night

Where will the brook lead us
As we follow it down the stream of life?
Where does it end?
In murky waters deep in the heart of nowhere,
Or on the quiet banks of the river
Of the dreamer's dreamless night?

How do we know which way to steer,
To find that quiet, that peace,
Where man meets his soul:
To ponder and reflect life's purpose,
To exist in nature itself
Where its reality brings us to the essence of life?

Life is a sea of realities
Knocking at the door.
Once opened, we are led thru' the currents of experience,
Tossed by the raging tumults,
Thru' the turmoil of our minds,
Gathering our treasures,
The secrets of our dreams;
Until we reach that quiet bank of the river
Where the dreamer's dreamless night
Becomes the bright reality of day.

(Until we become conscious of our beingness, we experience the dreamer's dreamless night. When we open the door of reality, our experiences and lessons give us the treasures of life, bringing us to the bright reality of day).

The Crossroads of Life

Life consists of a series of crossroads
Which we meet at intervals;
How we navigate each one
Determines the point at which
We meet the next.

At each crossroad
A major change
Or decision is required.

At each crossroad
An ending,
A new beginning,
    And the opportunity
    To determine the path
    We will tread.

At each crossroad
The choices are ours.

Our Beloved
(and so we meet again)

A Meditation!

In the Heart of the Soul of Man
Lies the very Essence of our Being;
So let us turn within
And touch that place
Where we become One
With all Life

For there,
In the very Heart of the Soul,
We meet our Beloved.

Oh yes! The pain of physical parting
Lies panting
Deep in our hearts:
What grief is endured
In such a loss.

But the beauty of the Spirit
Lives on,
Oh beloved!
In the whisper of the wind,
Hear her voice;
In the beauty of nature,
See her smile;
In the very essence of our Earth,
Feel Her Presence,
Oh Beloved!

So let us now withdraw
Into that inner world,
And be silent a while .
Listen,
To the silence;
Touch the very heart of your being.

Now step into the Temple
Of the Living God,
And from deep within,
Feel His Presence;
Rest in His comforting arms
As He embraces you
In His Love.

And there, in the stillness,
He guides us
Into the Heart of Life,
Where the Soul arises
To meet our Beloved.

Written as a special remembrance for my niece, in the knowledge that the spirit lives on in the 'World of Light' and that our loved one is with us always. Written words are not needed; we only need to turn within to the Heart of Life to meet our Beloved.

Dark Night of the Soul

Temptations and trials
Remain a source of experience
To the seeker;
  To bring a greater understanding,
  A deeper meaning,
  A closer union
  With the Infinite.

But, in the Dark Night of the Soul
Is the Supreme Test
Of Will, Mind,
Love, Faith and Trust;
  To bring the seeker
  To a higher state
  Of thought.

It is a time when the eyes are closed;
When the doors are shut;
And a mist appears.
There is darkness,
And the soul feels alone
In the wilderness:
  No Light,
  No Guide,
Just the knowledge
  Of Truth;
The experience
  Of Life;
And the memory
  Of the Inner Light.

Stumble around
In the darkness;
Look for the Way;
Look for the Light:
    Disillusionment:
    For there is none;
    You are left in the
    Dark Night of the Soul.

Where is my helper?
Where is the Light
That guides me?
Where is His Presence
To surround my Soul?

I am lost;
I am sad and tired;
I have tried so hard:
    Where is my God?

I want to scream;
I look to the world of pleasure:
    I cling a little;
    There is Hope:
    Can I see a glimmer of Light?

No!
Something tells me – 'No'!
'That is not the Way;
Remember your Creator'.

I struggle to remember,
But I cannot see;
The darkness surrounds me.

I sit in silence,
In meditation;
I try to feel
The Presence of God:
    There is nothing,
    Only the darkness.

The dawning breaks:
And in my memory
Of existence, I remember
    My lessons,
    My experiences,
    My knowledge;
And I know
I must travel
Through the darkness
Alone (in my illusion):
    Slowly, steadily;
    Trusting each step
    Is guided
    By the Great Spirit.

As I go on,
The darkness begins to lessen;
The air is lighter,
But I must tread slowly,
I must not stumble.

    (But I do):

        My mind is stayed on God
        Because I know
        His Light is there
        In the darkness.

I already feel
The Light Touch
Of His Presence;
And my heart grows lighter.

I already know
He is there,
Watching and waiting
For my soul
To emerge from the pit of despair.

I will tread slowly,
I must not stumble.

My thoughts are clearer,
I feel a new beginning;
I must prepare myself
For this higher state of mind,
To which I will emerge.

I must be ready
For at that time
I will awaken
To the significance
Of this experience
Of the Dark Night of My Soul.

The Awakening

To those who are on the spiritual path of Truth;
To those who are seeking Peace, Harmony, and Love;
The experience of The Infinite
In the awakening of the soul;
Read on:

The human mind is a torture unto itself;
Desiring earthly wants;
Love from those who know not love's meaning;
Truth from doubting minds;
Trust from those who trust not themselves;
Strength from the weak;
Harmony out of confusion; and
Peace from a world in turmoil.

Why turn to these souls?

The Soul Supreme
Awaits your Awakening:
To lead you out of the darkness,
Into the Fountain of Life;
Where, in the renewing of the spirit
A new found freedom,
An inner strength,
Will release your soul,
And reveal from the Mysteries,
The Truths of Life.

To Know Truth:

Remove all prejudice:
And with an open mind
The truth will unfold
In revelations and experiences
For your own understanding.

To Attain Harmony and Peace:

Search the depths of your innermost Being;
Severing all discord,
Clearing all adverse thoughts,
And, by instilling the Truth of your experiences
Deep into your conscience,
Harmony and Peace will grow.

To Experience the Infinite:

Sit in the Silence:
Let your mind unfold within;
And as the outward world grows dim,
You will unite with your Creator.

From this union,
Your soul will be awakened;
Your spirit will be renewed
In the Fountain of Life.
And Love, in its purity
Will grow within your being;
Unfolding to the Living Ether:

And in The Silence,
Your inner being will move
With the Breath of the Infinite,
Giving the Supreme Experience.

Soul Experience

I

In meditation
I await union with God;
And as His Presence surrounds me,
My soul is filled with His Love.

I I

Yet again
The disharmonies of life
Arrest my soul,
And I am left
Alone and confused.

Such experiences are many
That touch the harmony of my existence;
To impede my vision
As I grow in my awareness.

I am bewildered and confused,
Engulfed by the forces of darkness:
I am lost - deep in the pit of despair.
How can I survive?

I I I

At such times
Know that the negative forces surround you,
Leading your soul
Into oblivion.
Do not struggle
Or your confusion will grow
As your mind tries to reason;
Let yourself flow with its tide.

The roots of your being
Will be shaken
And His Light will dim for a while.

But remain steadfast:
    Always let the Eternal lie in your heart;
    For His Light is always there
    Beyond the darkness:
        And know
        That such forces
        Will pass away,
        Just as they came.

Remember this at all times,
For such experiences are many.
But as you overcome
They will get weaker;
And there will come a time
When your soul has matured
And you will remain
Forever in the Light
Where such forces cannot penetrate.

Then you will know
You are ever in the Presence of the Eternal:

    Your mind will be at peace;
    Your thoughts will be in harmony;
    Your heart will rest in love;
    And your soul will ever stay
    In the Light of the Eternal.

And There is Peace
(my concept of the World as it should have been)

I

The sky is blue,
The sun shines upon the Earth;
And there is Peace.

The sea is still,
Reaching out to the horizon;
And there is Peace.

When clouds appear
The rains will fall
And water the Earth,
To bring forth the fruits
In their season.

Night falls, stars twinkle
Through the darkness;
The moon gives out her light,
And there is Peace.

Seeds are planted:
The grass is green,
Flowers bloom,
Trees bear their fruit,
The harvest flourishes;
All is in abundance.

The animals are free,
A friend to man,
And there is Peace.

Man:
The highest of all creation;
Who tills the ground,
Who builds and creates
For the benefit of all.
Yes, there is Peace.

The Wise One,
Who leads the world in unity:
The Leaders are one,
The World is One.

For each man,
His home is the World.

From land to land we travel
To see the World;
No prohibiting laws,
The World is Ours.

The World is free
As God gave it free.

We all work for Her,
Using our talents
To bestow to the Whole;
And in return we receive
All that is our need.

Wherever we are,
In whatever part
Of this great creation,
All is equal for the needs of Man,
Animal and Nature.

All is free;
An abundance for eternity.
We all know it is not ours,
But His who made it.
So we share this World;

One country, one language,
All brothers, all friends.

In Unity, to share
What has been given,
Freely.

In Freedom we use it,
In Freedom we live,
And when departing,
'Tis left for those
Who come after;
For it is not ours,
But His Who created it.

We enter this World
With nothing
But Freedom.

Our lives
Having a purpose:

To experience and gain knowledge
Which is necessary for our development,
Leading to a deeper spiritual awareness
And growth
In preparation for Higher Planes.

And to the World:
We leave our mark
Of existence.

Is this a dream,
Or the reality of a World
Intended at the beginning of time?

II

Oh Man:
Your greed has brought you to shame:
For Beauty and Peace
You trade sin and war.

My heart is sad
At your misguided concepts of Life;
Not seeing beyond this World,
But only as far as the grave.

Think deep into your conscience;
We have a responsibility
To all creation:

Within us is the Light
Of our Creator.

To save ourselves
And the World
From destruction,
Let us sit a while

And meditate:

Love unites;
And with Unity
Comes Freedom.

Let us learn to Love;
Let us Unite;
Let us all be Free:

For this is not just a dream,
But the reality of a World
That should have been:

AND THERE WILL BE PEACE.

Depression

From the roots of one's being
It weighs heavily upon the heart,
Penetrating the mind:
Blurring vision,
Confusing thought,
Hindering action,
Subduing the Will.

The sweetness of life is forgotten
As it soars through every vein;
The spirit falling to its lowest ebb,
Giving way to unreasoning thoughts,
And doubting the existence of
The Source of Life.

But to every soul that suffers
A Light will shine;
A Whisper will sound:

With an open heart,
See that Light;
With a willing ear,
Hear that Whisper.

And through the darkness,
In the depths of depression;
A ray of hope will flicker;
Words of comfort heard:
To know there's always a Listener
Who understands
And cares

The Whirlwind

I feel as if I have been
Travelling thru' a whirlwind
Which has left me
In total disarray
In mind, body and soul.

For as I struggled
To maintain my state of
Peace, Harmony and Balance,
The winds of change
Swept thru' my world
Carrying me on a journey

Of experiences
Which took me out of my space
Into that of others.

And now,
As I observe myself
I am reminded
Of the sanctity of 'self'.
Of that sacred place
Where the soul abides.

For the winds of change
Will often sweep thru' our world
Like a whirlwind
Uprooting our life
In unexpected and sometimes difficult ways
Bringing new kinds of experiences and lessons
Ready to uplift us
Into greater heights of understanding
And Grace.

So wherever we are,
In whatever space,
We must maintain our balance,
Our sacred place
Of 'self'.

Seasons of Life

As the leaves fall
In the dusk of the autumn winds,
I ponder,
And am filled with awe
At life's ebb and flow
In all things.

As the seasons
Bring forth their fruit,
So they recede in slumber.

Our lives
Have their seasons
        Of joy and sadness,
        Loneliness and fear,
        Of love and beauty,
        Of life and rebirth.
Where nature
Works out its plan
Throughout the universe.

Nature

Imagine green fields
With blossoming trees;
Green branches lean over
The buds beneath;
The wildest of flowers
Array the earth:
    In nature – His Wonders fulfilled.

Look up to the sky,
Not a cloud is in sight;
Its blueness – a glimpse at infinity;
The sun shines through,
Giving light to the day:
    In nature – His Wonders fulfilled.

Imagine the valleys
Where mountains rise high;
Streams rippling below,
With banks running by:
    In nature – His Wonders fulfilled.

God breathes in nature;
God breathes out His Love:
    In nature – His Love is fulfilled.

The Countryside

I long for the peace and quiet of the countryside,
Wherein its shelter I may hide
Myself into its bosom shield;
My soul unto its beckoning yield.

In its fullness it holds a deep tranquillity,
Flooding through earth's serenity;
So its beauty unfolds each hour,
As do the buds of a flow'r.

The green fields stretch for miles around,
          Its stillness
Captures my heart;
Yielding to enraptures
Its beauty endows upon me,
The peace of eternity.

The Sky

The sky leads to the vast expanse of space;
          The universe;
God, the Creator of all.

The sky is blue when the sun shines,
'Tis grey when the clouds descend;
And in the darkness of the night
It looms upon us.

Yet, with the twinkling of the stars,
And the brightness of our moon,
We can gaze upon the sky
With wonder;
And seek to understand
That we're a part of this creation,
And marvel.

Look, and see its wonders;
Listen, and hear its whisperings of truth;
Reach out, and feel its closeness.

We belong
Not to one world,
But to all worlds:
Look to the sky
And know.

The Sea

Look to the sea,
'Tis calm;
Our souls are filled with peace;
The harmony of the world
As it should have been.

The waves rock to and 'fro,
Our hearts beat to its rhythm,
Our bodies swaying with its motion,
Moving with the Soul of the world.

The waters stretch to the horizon,
And our souls reach out
To rest in the tranquillity
Of the sea.

The Sea
(at night)

Calm,
In the night,
As the moon gives her light.
Glistening,
Like gold,
As the night doth unfold.
Still,
No sound;
The silence rebounds.

Peaceful,
Is the sea,
In its tranquillity.

We Serve
(Written for Brian and all Light / Peace Workers)

We all choose our path thru' life;
For some, it is a path of service,
To help make a difference
In some way (however small),
To bring harmony and peace to humanity.

The essence of our chosen way
Is the Love, Light, Harmony and Peace
Which flows from our hearts
To those
Who will hear its Truths.

Yet the hardships we experience
In opening that part of ourselves
To reach the hearts and minds
Of those we touch
Can be difficult to bear.
For the 'human' mind'
May not always be ready
To embrace our hand of peace.

So we must remember
As we quietly continue our way,
That we are not alone.
For as we each pour out our love
In service
For the uplifting of mankind,
So we create a chain of Light
Which unites us.

Turn within
And sit in quiet contemplation:
Feel the power of that web of Light
Which links us thru' our heart centres.

And from the Source of all Life,
The comfort,
And whisperings of Love
Will surround us,
Giving us the courage to go on.

And know:
Every heart we touch
Brings us nearer the time when
Love and Light will fill the earth,
Thru' the hearts and souls
Of humanity:

And there will be Peace.

The Healing Richness of Life

As I sit in meditation,
With the Light of Life
Filling my whole being,
My Guardians and the Angels
Encircle about me:
I am at Peace.

Then, without warning,
Painful reminders from my past
Present themselves
To disturb my tranquillity;
And I ask, "why".

Yet it is just in this setting
Of Love, Light and Peace,
That we are able to help ourselves
Come to terms with past experiences and emotions.
For as they rise up
From the depths of our consciousness,
Embraced in Love and Light,
They dissolve into the ether,
And become Light.

And so,
As we absorb
The Light of our experiences
In our understanding of Life's lessons,
We heal ourselves
In the richness of Life.

MEMORIES
(Written in memory of my niece, Sola)

Memories
Lie in the silence of the heart,
In the stillness of the air.
And the fleeting wind that blows
Carries the breath and the sighs
Of all life,
Of all our memories.

As we listen to the stillness;
In each breath of the universe,
We hear the whispers of life;
The heartbeat of the memories,
And feel the eternity of time.

It is in this stillness,
The eternal stillness,
We remember and know
The meaning of life.

For God, in all His mercy
Gave us the beauty of memories,
The gift of love,
To hold in our hearts,

(Until the eternal call
Re-unites all souls).

Sola,
Your beautiful memory
Never fades in our hearts.
And when we hear God's call
We will join you
In eternity.

Life's Lessons
(written for my daughter - Priscilla)

I

Be thankful for the lessons
We learn on our journey through life,
For the people we meet along the way,
And for the help and guidance we receive
On our long and arduous path.

Some lessons may be difficult;
We may stumble many a time;
But with patience, and a gentle guiding hand
We are always given the opportunity
To try again.

It is not easy
This road through life;
It is filled with pain and hardship,
Sorrow and grief.

But we are here to learn these lessons,
And when, on that day, we understand
The meaning of such things,
We will gather the strength
To do that which is required,
And raise ourselves up
To meet the demands made upon us.

II

Each soul we meet
Has a message, a lesson, for our own development;
See each relationship
As a gift from God;
For in this you will find
The Blessings of Life:
Love, Humility, Wisdom.

And on that day we understand
The part each soul plays
In the Music of Life,
We can then place each soul
In his/her rightful place
In our hearts and in our lives.

So, as we grow
In Humility, Grace and Wisdom,
We receive more strength and understanding
From the Source of all Life
To keep us moving forward on our path.

III

And thus, with each step,
Comes the slow dawning
Of the Beauty of this Life:
    Where each soul,
    As it grows in Wisdom,
    Abounds with Divine Love,
    Humility, Harmony, and Peace.

My Prayer for Help

Help me oh Lord
To live the life I desire,
To be what I yearn to be,
    'A Light within Life'.

    A beacon that shines on the hill,
    Lighting the way for all who pass by.

Oh Lord, help me
To bring out the love
That is within me;
To grow in wisdom
And help my fellow man.

Help me Lord,
To rise above all pettiness
Of the outer mind,
And see the beauty of the spirit
In all things.

No Regrets

We think tomorrow will be a better day,
Or next year a better year;
Then, on looking back,
We wonder:

    The error of that day.
    The errors of lost years,
    And tears
    Of regret.

Wipe those tears,
Linger not on regret,
For yesterday has gone:

    The events of yesterday
    Form our thoughts for today,
    Which mould our experiences of tomorrow.

So ponder on such thoughts
That will make a better tomorrow;
For the time of tomorrow is today,
And our thoughts of today
Become the way of tomorrow:
    And the way of tomorrow
    Are the events of yesterday.

Through positive thoughts,
Tomorrow will be a better day;
Through positive action,
Next year will be a better year;

And when looking back,
See the errors of time
As lessons learned
For a better tomorrow.

And no tears,
No regrets;
But a smile
As understanding grows
Through the knowledge gained.

Facing My Fear

When you know the time is right,
In complete surrender to God
With trust in His Love
And clothed in Divine Light
Unlock the recesses of your mind,
Open up the gates of your heart
And enter the depths of your soul
To meet what lies hidden
From your 'self';

Do not fear the unknown
Do not fear what lies waiting
For in your fear it gains its strength,
It gains its power
And grows.

Sit in the silence with God,
Let the hidden emerge
Clothed in Divine Light,
Strong within His arms
In Peace and Love,

Watch your fear rise up,
Let it make itself known
And face-to-face you will meet
What?
An illusion you have created
From your fear of the 'unknown'
To find it shrinks to dust
When confronted to present itself.

So be strong dear soul;
Face your fear,
Make room for the Light.
Let it fill the recesses of your mind
To enter the gates of your heart
And fill the depths of your soul.

Partners in Life

Partnerships are built on trust,
On friendship, love and respect
For one another.

How long a partnership will last
Will depend upon several factors:
For we are all souls
On our personal journey thru' life.
We come together as our paths merge,
To help each other
On our way.

So where we differ,
We must try to understand
Those differences,
And why they affect us.

This can create many difficulties.
But it is a two-way affair:
Giving and receiving,
Understanding and empathy,
Change and growth;
Meeting each other half way.

Yet sometimes the trials may overcome us,
And the differences too diverse.
And we find that all has been
A stepping stone - a part of our growth,
To provide the foundation
For our future relationships.

Yet where we are able
To resolve our differences,
We become stronger in that partnership;
With a deeper love and respect
Which only time,
And the experiences of life,
Can provide.

So remember,
Be thankful for all life's lessons and experiences;
The positive and the negative,
For they are blessings bestowed upon us
For our growth,
As we gain wisdom, humility and grace.

Keith Clarke Holgate

Keith was born in Burnley, Lancashire on 5 March 1937, a true Pisces – a charismatic, compassionate, kind, caring, romantic, loving person.
Unlike other collections within this anthology, the inclusion of Keith's poetry acts as a posthumous dedication to the love that Keith had for his wife Annette, his two sons (Dean, aged 37, and James, aged 27yrs) and his extended family. It was while Keith was conducting business abroad (from around 1992) that he started to send home poems to his wife, who kept them safe.
The last poem that Keith wrote by hand was written two months prior to his passing, entitled *Love and Light and Angels Dear*, the words of which are on the headstone of his grave.
Keith passed away on 20 December 2002 following a battle against a belated diagnosis of leukaemia. Forever the optimist, Keith truly believed that he'd recover – even playing cricket for Shepperton Cricket Club in the September of that year.
Another side of Keith that not many people knew about was that he was an intuitive and psychic. Annette and Keith felt mutually sure that they had been together in previous lives and had experienced several spiritual synchronicities during their life together. He understood about the power of healing and was a trained reiki healer. Keith supported and encouraged Annette in her training to becoming an aromatherapist, reflexologist, and reiki master. At the end, Annette hoped that their belief in the Light and Angels would guide him in his passing. While she was sitting in the hospital chapel just after Keith's death, he spoke to her saying that he was in a place of light, surrounding by many 'radiant faces', and Wanda (his beautiful dog), who was so pleased to see him again.
Annette used to joke with Keith that one day she'd get his poems published. It seems, however, that Keith had not quite

finished sending her poetry following his passing into the spirit realms. During a psychic gathering, Teresa Larkin channelled a poem, *My Darling Wife*, from Keith to Annette. Ros Knight of Market Harborough transcribed the poem as it was *read* through Teresa.

My Darling Wife

We have journeyed down the road of happy memories
And gazed at the starlit sky at night,
We have shared deep love for one another
And your heart was my ray of light.

You would greet me with your loving smile
And fill my life with your happiness,
You have always been my diamond -
With you I was truly blessed.

Now you feel life's taken me from you
And you can't bear the journey any longer,
But just for me, my diamond light,
Could you be a little stronger?

For this world, it needs your presence
There's work on earth for you to do,
And, my love, you're not alone
For I am walking right beside you.

So while I'm here
Please wear the smile I've loved for many years,
It's time to face the future now -
Bring me laughter; dry your tears.

Let's be thankful, you and I,
For many blessings came our way,
Just hold your head up to the sun
And find within that brighter day.

You will feel my presence near you -
And in your heart you will hear my song.
So much love we still can share
So, just for me, please be strong.

Take my hand my darling
Our hearts are still together,
There is no separation -
We will journey on forever.

Listen, for I am calling you
Let our spirits dance and entwine,
As you walk on in your world
And I, my love, in mine.

I will be your candlelight
In dark times to help you see,
I will be your sunshine
And bring my warmth to thee.

I will be your strength
Each and every day,
For I am walking with you
To help you on your way.

So walk with me with smiles
Upon a path of happiness,
Lift those sorrows from your heart
For we are truly blessed.

So raise your head my darling
And greet each day with cheer,
Knowing that I am with you -
There's no need for you to fear.

For life to you is calling -
So much you have to give,
Take my sunshine into your heart
And show others how to live.

Shine in them our light
All those lost within their pain,
And we will be a comfort to them
To help them live again.

Keith channelled this poem through the mediumship of Teresa Larkin in February 2004. Ros Knight of Market Harborough transcribed the poem as it was channelled.

A Special Day

A clear blue sky, sunlight bright
A reprise of long ago
When we were young and so in love,
Our faces all aglow.

This day so many years ago
Was special for us both
The day we would unite in love
The day we would betroth.

A ring slipped on a trembling finger
To complete the vows we made
I held your hand so tenderly
Our love would never fade.

Throughout the years just you and I
Have faced the tests of life
Together we have had the strength
To overcome the strife.

So many years have flown on by
That day seems far away
But time will not erode our love
Together we will stay.

On that day we took our vows
One thing I know is true
That all I longed for long ago
Was no-one else but you.

Thoughts

Thinking of you in the light of day
Thinking of you as I go my way
Thinking of you as the evening approaches
Thinking of you in a garden of roses

Just thinking of you makes the absence easy to bear
My thoughts are my presence, reach out, I am there.

The Friendship of a Flower

The loneliness of life
When lovers are apart
Is gladdened by the scent of flowers,
Sent with feelings from the heart.

The blossoms dance, weave their spell
Of magic and mystique
I need your love and gentleness
To make my life complete.

Born on the Wind

Wind through the trees
Wind from above
Caresses the garden
That I'm thinking of.

For now it's a dream
But soon I'll be there
Born on the wind
To whisper, "I care."

Across the Sea

Across the sea, how far, how far
I see you now from yonder star
I blow you a kiss from over the blue
For you my love, only for you.

The years roll by but we should say,
"I love you" every single day.

Time is but a fleeting glance
Of the life and love we shared by chance.

And now my thoughts wing across the sea
For no-one else, but you and me.

Precious Time

Time is there for everyone
A breath of wind for all to share
A walk by sunlit woods and streams
Brings joy beyond compare.

This time so precious to us all
In a moment it can fade
As life and love just ebb away
In silence, Heaven made.

Love Always

Miss me dear
As I miss you
Morn and evening
Night time too.

The miles may
Keep us far apart
But love is always
In my heart.

A love so rare
So strong, so true
The answer simply,
I love you.

LUV – YOU

Think of me in the clouds so high
I'll be thinking of you as the miles drift by
Then as you drift into the valley of sleep
Lock my love in your heart; it's yours to keep.

Love and Light and Angels Dear

Love and light and angels dear
Nothing there for you to fear
For they will guide you to peace and rest
Forever loved and Heaven blessed

You can be sure on this special day
That I am never far away
From all the things I know are true
My love, my life, are just for you

Angels in the mist of life
Are always there for you
So listen, feel and understand
And make your dreams come true

To Live is to Love

To live is to love
On this most special day
Know that, "I love you"
Is all I can say.

Our love binds us closely,
Even when we're apart,
But today I can tell you
What's here in my heart.

It's simple, it's true
And to give you a clue
The love that I have
Is love, just for you.

To age is to live
To live is to love
I send you my love
On the wings of a dove.

It takes but a moment
To say, "I love you"
But the echo remains
Until life is through.

Think of Me

As the morning sun
Awakes the sea
Think of me

As the waves break gently
Over the golden sand
Think of me

As tropical palms
Bow their respect to the wind
Think of me

As sunbeams
Dance across a sparkling sea
Think of me

Then as the evening comes
And all is still,
With moonlight softly beaming,
My thoughts will fly to you alone
Should you be awake, or maybe dreaming

As darkness then completes the day
It would be nice to be
Out there with you among the stars and by
An azure sea.

I think of you
You think of me
So far away across the sea

With thoughts as one
I'm always near
So speak my name
And I'll be here

Sleep warm and let
The angels keep
A watch for me, but
Do not peep.

Higher, Deeper

High up in the sky above
My thoughts turn to the ones I love
So far below, beneath the clouds
Amongst the earthbound moving crowds

My loved ones seem so lost from view
But still my thoughts are seeking you
To tell you all that while I'm gone
My love for you goes on and on

Higher than the highest mountain
Deeper than the deepest sea
These highs and lows can all be reached
If you believe in me.

From the Edge

Once more

Her lovely face comes into view
A joy for me to see
Back from the edge of eternity
To spend more time with me

I love her so, my cherished girl
So gentle yet so strong
She fills my life with love and light
Ever close when things go wrong

To walk her in the sunlight
Or on a cloudy day
Always my close companion
As we go along our way

I look into her loving eyes
As she turns her head to me
They tell me all I want to know
She is happy, plain to see

We walk along, sun going down
Together, homeward bound
I pat her gently, stroke her brow
As she gently paws the ground

Evening time, she cuddles close
So tired, yet content
She lays her head upon my lap
Her being Heaven sent

As she is walked the path of darkness
I feared that we would part
She saw my sadness and returned
To heal my broken heart.

To my beautiful Wanda, my companion through all adversity

SIAM … the Cat

Soft as a snowflake,
White as the snow,
I came into your life.
My stay was brief,
But in my time
I knew you loved me so

The garden was my jungle,
The walls my mountain lair,
What fun I had on sunlit days
In my world beyond compare

And then as twilight touched the sky,
My day's adventures through,
I laid my body down to rest
As always, close to you

My life so short - I wonder why
My days were soon ended,
But what must be must always be
And sorrow can be mended

To know I brought some joy to you
Has made my life complete
Remember me with tenderness
As I lie in silent sleep

I am There

Think of me when lights are low,
When darkness fills the air.
Think of me and for a while
Pretend that I am there,

For I will think of you each night
When darkness fills the air.
Think of me and for a while
Pretend that I am there,

For I will think of you each night
While you are far away,
And send my love on dancing stars
To warm you night and day

Enjoy the sun and sand and sea,
The daytime and the night.
Enjoy the time and space you find,
Surrounded by the light.

The light of love shines bright for us -
I'm sure you are aware
Of the precious time we have as one
In our world beyond compare

My Brother

Dean, my brother, tall and slim,
His life's so full of fun.
He likes to drive and swim and jog
And sometime shoot his gun.

His gun is silver, light and neat
With bullets made of plastic.
He moves around the shooting range
As though he were elastic.

Inners, outers - all shots count
But some are wide and bad.
Two bull's eyes in a shooting match
Was the best he'd ever had.

He's twenty-three, blonde and strong.
To know him makes me glad.
He *wheels and deals* in many things -
They call him *Jack the Lad*

Soon he is off to the USA -
Helicopter lessons he will face.
I wonder if he'll think of me
While spinning round in space?

I miss him, how I miss him,
The days seem so much longer.
But all the time he is away
Our bond becomes much stronger.

Happy Birthday Messages

Across the ocean wild and wide
Comes this birthday wish for you,
To tell you that I miss you so
With a love so warm and true.

How soon the days will fly on by
Until we meet again,
And then I'll whisper in your ear,
"Happy birthday darling" as I step down from the plane

And so for now a kiss I blow
Out into time and space,
Across the starry night it flies -
Can you feel it touch your face?

~o~

A birthday is a happy day,
Especially spent with me.
Where else would you wish to be -
Perhaps down by the sea?

But the sea is such a lonely place -
Cold and wet and deep.
Here in the shelter of my arms
Your day will be complete.

The night draws near, the day is done,
Birthday almost through,
But what a joy it's been to me
To spend this day with you

Tomorrow is another day,
Birthday joy is over.
A little older, it is true,
But still my perfect luvver!

~o~

Angels in the midst of life
Are always there for you,
So listen, feel and understand,
And make your dreams come true.

Happy Birthday, Luvver and the Angels

Valentine

I may be old and I may be grey,
But you are in my thoughts today.
My valentine you will always be -
There's no-one but you, that's plain to see.

Tricia Sturgeon

Patricia lives in Mundesley, Norfolk and has been writing poetry for many years, having a diverse portfolio of themes. Se has featured on local radio with some of her poetry and has also had some poems published in magazines.
A prolific writer, Tricia says that she feels that the poetry just 'comes through' – that it is 'given to her'.
Some of Tricia's poetry is reminiscent of the Stanley Holloway-style monologue and remembers some by heart. Other poems are like fantastical bedtime stories, yet many are deeply spiritual and philosophical in their content.

You Tell me You See Fairies

You tell me you see fairies…
Watch them whirl and twirl and fly.
You say I do not see them 'cause
They're very, very shy
And very, very magical
And very, very wise,
And only ever show themselves
To wide and wondering eyes.
If I sit still beside you,
Why then, I may just catch
Their game of Tag or Hide and Seek
Down by the cabbage patch.

All are clad in spider silk
Newly spun at dawn;
One has just washed out her wings
And looks a bit forlorn.
Their laughter rings like bluebells,
Their smiles are sunbeam bright,
They play and play the whole day long
And never, ever fight.
By night, they gather moonbeams
All shiny, new and clean,
To weave a silver coronet -
A gift for Mab, their Queen.
They dip it in a rainbow
So it shines with every hue
Then spangle it with diamonds
Gleaned from the morning dew.

And elves are mounted on their steeds
Field mice, sleek and brown
Riding forth to gather in
Bags of thistledown,
To stuff the tiny pillows
And the duvets, soft and deep,
To keep the fairies cosy
When they snuggle down to sleep.

You tell me you see fairies
Where I see leaf and stalk.
I hear the wind a-whistling
But you hear fairy talk.
There has to be a reason
And the reason has to be
That I'm a grown up mummy
And you are only three,
And 'ere you leave your childhood
As, little one, you must.
I hope that they will sprinkle you
With silver fairy dust,
Then, with years flown and you all grown
Perhaps, yourself a wife,
You will always see the magic
In the cabbage patch of life.

Transformation

There's a path that leads to nowhere
At the bottom of the lane,
Ending in a patch of common ground,
Where piles of garden rubbish
Find their final resting place
In ugly, tangled, twisted, withered mound -
Uncared for and untended -
An eyesore and a dump,
A blot upon the landscape. A disgrace.
N birds, no bees, no butterflies,
No creatures of the field,
No, nothing lived, I that benighted place.

Till Nature, taking pity,
On the sad, neglected spot,
Called upon her fairies and her sprites
To sprinkle it with magic and
To weave a spell or two,
Filled with joy and wonder and delight.
And there, one sunny morning,
I beheld heir handiwork,
Fair as any cultivated plot
Spangled o'er with daisies,
Dipped in dandelion gold,
With, here and there, a shy forget-me-not.
All wrapped round with poppies
And garlanded with light
A vibrant chord in earth's sublime refrain…
A little bit of Eden, located just beyond
The path that leads to nowhere
At the bottom of the lane.

Alchemy

Since suns have set
And oceans rolled
Mankind has sought,
So we are told,
For secrets which
Bright stars foretold,
The magic which
Turns base to gold.

Pale sorcerers,
Magicians wise,
Winged wizards who
Traverse the skies,
Are searching for
That precious prize
But looking through
Unseeing eyes.

When sunbeams warm
The sleeping earth
And blackbird sings
For all he's worth
To welcome spring
Proclaim the birth
Of beauty, hope
And joy and mirth.

When gold adorns
Bright shrub and tree
And buttercups grow
Wild and free

Spreading far
As eye can see
That's alchemy enough for me.

Put Out The Stars

Supremacy of intellect
Places Man, it seems
First in all Creation
And architect of dreams
Doctor, lawyer, preacher
Politician, engineer
Pushing back the boundaries
Of ignorance and fear.

Build it bigger, build it better
Build it higher, clear the ground
Raze the forest, dig the meadow
Never pause to look around.
Keep on moving. Time is money.
What you get is what you earn
No commercial value…
No commission, no return.
Growth and progress. On-line banking,
Self improvement - find out how
You too can make a million
Have it all and have it now.
Play the markets, make a killing,
Buy yourself a brand new face,
For it's Devil take the hindmost
When you're in the human race.

Put out the stars, close veil the sun
And make a deal with Death
To stand, unmoved as stone, as earth
Draws slow and laboured breath,
While the fine and wondrous balance
Which embraces sea and land
Is choked and violated by
That intellectual hand.

Discovery

Each body is a wonderful creation
Of flesh and blood, or sinew, bone and nerve,
Intricately woven into fabric
And given shape with height and width and curve.

Complete with brain to orchestrate the movement
Of all the merry molecules of life,
And heart to pump, and send them on their journey
To nourish, build and heal through joys and strife.

Are they the sum of this amazing structure?
Does the hardware and the software make the whole?
For wither consciousness in this equation
And is there room somewhere to hide a soul?

And if there is, and if it is eternal,
Surviving when all else is turned to dust
Does it hover, seeking further habitation
Or fly towards the Source, in hope and trust?

There, will it find a love that's all-embracing
A deep enfolding and a "Welcome home".
Inscribing all it learned whilst incarnated
In some forever, vast Akashic tome?

Then, will we know that each is part of the other
And all are One and all Divinely blessed?
If this be so, then there lies understanding,
For soul-less, there's no meaning in the rest.

Crossing the Void

There is a bridge that spans untold dimensions
'Tis woven of the love within the heart
Spun throughout the living of a lifetime
That souls may ne'er be sundered and apart

It rises out of swirling mists of longing
And, strong enough to bear all grief and pain,
Bears travellers across the darkest chasms
To join with all those dearly loved again.

For mind and soul traverse all mortal confines
To dwell within Eternity unbound
Reality expands to new horizons
And all that once was lost can now be found

Take but one step … see, here's a star to guide you
Be not afraid, the bridge is very real
'Twill take you out of black, despairing darkness
Into that Light, where broken hearts may heal.

Divergent Paths

Do not waste the precious hours with weeping
Nor squander time in yearning or regret.
Don't hold my soul in thrall with bitter longing
Or seek to join me 'ere your goals are met.

Whilst heart and mind are torn with grief and anguish
And days have lost all purpose, joy and flow,
Mortality obscures that high decision
Made on other spheres, aye long ago.

That I would make my exit from this drama
So you might walk, a little while, alone
And face the consequence of such a parting,
A lonely darkness, hitherto unknown.

So go, dear heart, and do not fear the journey
Just grasp life's hand, and hold on very tight.
Brave your deepest fears, and inner shadows
And I will be your star. Your guiding light.

The Last Mystery

What will become of you, and what of me
When dark Death comes to claim us as his own?
Will there be some spark at last set free
To join the flame, all knowing and all known?

Suppose this Death comes as a thief, a vandal,
To snatch all hope and desecrate the whole…
Will I then be snuffed out like a candle,
Extinguished? Just a body with no soul?

Will there be a wandering, seeking, waiting,
Looking for the pathway to re-birth?
Or will there be a coming home, a sating
With everything once hungered for on earth?

Will there be all or else will there be nothing?
No sleep. No dream. Oblivion … or life…
A longing for reuniting, joyous rushing
To outstretched arms of mother, brother, wife?

Ah, will there be a loving and a knowing,
A harvesting, a reaping what was sown?
Will there be warmth and nurturing and growing,
Will love survive and wait and find its own?

Whatever then be mortal's final fate
Lies secret-stored until the veil is rest,
When that which you've become, awaits me too
It cannot be so. I am content.

All Together Now…

Every single second,
Every heartbeat tick of Time,
Encapsulates the whole of life
In holographic mime.
Myriad new beginnings
Draw their expectant breath,
As endings make their exit
In this dance of Life and Death.

Desert sands. Gentle rain.
Motorway. Country Lane.
Crushing loss. Massive gain.
Soaring wings. Rusty chain.

Helping hand. Miser's clutch.
Running wild. Tiny hutch.
Vicious blow. Tender touch.
Mass starvation. Much too much.

Rainbow hopes. Black despair.
Crass neglect. Loving care.
Devastation. All set fair.
Hoard and stockpile. Care and share.

Like the clicking of a shutter,
Or the blinking of an eye,
Each action is recorded,
Every word and every sigh,
Past the understanding, beyond the asking why.
Captured all together
As Eternity goes by.

Apocalypse

A planetary symphony is ringing out in space,
But sad to tell, this harmony is flawed.
For the ego-led vibrations of the care-less human race
Cause Earth to strike a harsh and strident chord.

All lust filled greed for power, each blinkered grasping thought
The cruelty that rips and tears apart,
And every bomb exploded and every battle fought
Resonate to Earth's great beating heart.

Causing there, a wounding and a deep, abiding grief
That all her wondrous gifts are sore abused,
While each tormented creature and every withered leaf
Bear testament to clemency refused.

Now the tempo's getting quicker and the sands are running out
And the chance to turn around may soon be gone
And what price power and glory then, and who's the final shout?
When Earth is charred and blackened and the orchestra plays on?

Memories

For just a little while we have the power,
Given at the moment of our birth,
To manifest the care of the Creator
Upon these darkly shadowed plains of earth.

Only for the spanning of a lifetime,
Be that long, or tiny-heartbeat short,
We may touch the essence of another
And gift away the love that we have brought.

With passing years, the soul may not remember
Those larger realms, eternal and divine,
From whence it came. And be content to linger
And feast on coarser bread and lesser wine.

Thus we may use up the hours and minutes,
The days and months of our allotted time,
Wrapped within a dark cocoon of doing,
Doubting there's a reason in the rhyme.

Until some yearning, shuttered by the senses,
Breaks illusion's bonds, to rise in flight,
Awakening a deep subconscious knowing
That all are One, and Life is Love and Light.

Elemental

Somewhere within the very deepest deep of me,
Guarded by the beating of my heart,
There glows a tiny flickering of knowing
That I will ever be a living part
Of this great, pulsating, shining cosmos,
Where energies vibrate and change and grow
In cavalcades of make-belief and magic.
An ever new and never ending show.

A tapestry of light and sound and colour,
Growing and evolving with each strand.
Following a blueprint which could only
Spring from some Divine Creative Hand.
And yet…and here's the marvel, here's the wonder…
In all this vast, amazing panoply,
Every soul is cherished and beloved
And held in All That Is, and is to be.

Magic

If I could find a magic wand
I'd wave it in the air,
And cast a spell to take away
All fear and pain and care.
I'd clear the dark and stormy clouds,
Revealing skies of blue,
And smooth the rocks, which mar the path
For you and you and you.

I'd feed the starving, heal the sick
And bid all conflicts cease,
So every heart could feel awhile
The blessed balm of peace.

But wands, alas, are hard to find.
I don't have one to hand,
And dreams of solving worldly ills
Are spun of shifting sand.
So each must use the stuff of life,
The losses and the gains,
To weave a rainbow coloured robe,
Or heavy laden chains.
And, toiling thus, from day to day,
Assuredly we'll find
The magic's in the mixing
Of the heart and soul and mind.

Seasons

There was a time when
    You were all my life
        My waking thought, my daily bread,
        Possessing heart and soul and head.
        My hope, my fear. My Deity.
        My now and my eternity.
    Spring fever running rife.

A time when
Love could do no wrong
For sweet, swift hours were dream imbued,
And all the world was rainbow hued.
Stars shed luminescent lights
O'er wild, impassioned, scented nights.
While earth sang summer's song.

A time when
The carousel stood still
And only silent music played.
Indifference crept in…and stayed.
Love chains gave way to rusty key
The coloured leaves fell off the tree
And autumn's winds blew chill.

Now comes a time when
Blood runs cold and thin
And solitary steps admit
Twilight hours are lonely lit
Harsh Time cleaves furrows on the brow
I would not have you see me now,
As winter closes in.

New Years Eve

Whilst church bells chime
Swift sands of Time
Build castles, high in the air.
And the heart and the mind
Are briefly inclined
To soar, and inhabit them there.

As memories crowd,
All clamouring loud
Of days which have gone before,
Full of hope and of fear,
It is suddenly clear
We have reached a revolving door.

And, standing again
In that empty frame
To the future, the present, the past,
Illusions play is swept away
Revealing the truth at last.

I am you. You are me.
In this great cosmic sea,
In which all creation's afloat
And all pleasures and pains
Are but pearls on the chain
Adorning Eternity's throat.

The Home Straight

The days are getting shorter now,
The sun is not so high.
The grass that grows across the fence
Less green, and rather dry.
Sweet Youth looks very young indeed,
Yet also very wise.
And Eternity seems nearer than
The wide and empty skies.

The images are not so sharp
All sounds are turned down low
Yet colours hold a vibrancy
A deep and inner glow.
The heart of Life beats slowly, like
A velvet-muffled drum,
And years a-waiting in the wings
May simply never come
Yet everything has settled down
Into it's rightful place
Within the Universal Arms.
And I am touched by Grace

Never Too Late

There may come a time, when you say to yourself
"How on earth did I get to this place…
So littered with rubbish and pitted with holes
That I fear I'll fall flat on my face
And all around there's a choking fog
Sucking the life from the day
I daren't go forward and cannot go back
For I burned every bridge on the way
Loudly proclaiming my right to pursue
My pleasures, wherever they led
But they brought me here and left me alone
With a wasteland inside of my head."

If this is your song, take heart my friend,
For you see, it is never too late
To have a few words with the Universe,
Requesting a change in your fate.
Look deep in the depths of your aching heart,
Acknowledge the emptiness there,
Then, feeling the warmth of Eternal arms,
Reach for a wing, with a prayer.
Ask for a star to lighten your way,
And a hand to hold as you go,
Let seeds of hope take root in your heart
And watch all those miracles grow.

Signs and Miracles

They say that wondrous miracles
Took place in times long past.
They do not happen now, of course
With life so full and fast.
For folk who used to see them were
The plain and simple kind.
Such wonders have no place inside
The clever, modern mind.

But friends, I beg to differ
With everything *they* say.
For miracles are happening
Around us every day.
It's just that they're so commonplace
They slip by all unseen,
Light shadows in the moonlight
And youth, at sweet sixteen.

For instance, when the evening drapes
Her shawls of darkest grey,
I press a switch upon the wall
And lo…'tis bright as day,
As pearly globes of glass light up
With incandescent glow.
I don't know how it happens
But I'm very glad it's so.
And even though I'm by myself
I feel no loneliness.
The reason? Why, a miracle
(As if you couldn't guess)

For, should I feel the need to chat
At any time of day
Why then I simply "phone a friend"
Nearby or far away.

Drama, laughter, news and sport
They're all right there for me,
Miraculously tucked away
Inside my old TV.
Snowdrops breaking winter earth
Seabirds flying free,
Scented summer roses
Light full autumn tree.
Icicles and snowflakes,
Drumming, dancing rain.
Seedlings sown in March
Gold September grain.
Families and friendships,
Something in the air,
Miracles and wonders
Simply everywhere.
Now they may say "It's science"
Or "It's nature" but you see
The truth's in the beholding…
They are miracles to me.

Oh God…!

I do not understand a God
Whose fixed and iron will
Decrees that faithful followers
Must hurt and main and kill.
I do not understand a God
Who twists the heart and mind,
Demanding slavish duties from
The blind, led by the blind.
A God who's quick to take offence,
To blame, to hold a grudge,
Bereft of all compassion
And a swift and cruel judge.

A God like that could only spring
From Man's poor little brain,
Obsessed with power and progress,
And all things trite and vain.
Ignoring simple truths which all
The sacred writings hold,
That love alone unlocks the code,
Which turns the base to gold.
So Man must make his destiny,
Be that for good or ill,
For he accepted long ago
A precious gift…free will…

To walk the path of vengeance
And bigotry and blood
And hell-fire and damnation,
Famine, fire and flood.

Or else to take the upward road,
Which sets the self apart
And leads, through Understanding
To Love's creative heart.
If we could just aspire to be
As God-like as we can,
Instead of making the Divine
Resemble paltry man…

Then, perhaps, and only then
Would wars and conflicts cease,
And Earth draw breath, and sing at last
Of universal peace.

Giving

How you can say you have nothing to give,
No riches to scatter abroad?
No soaring talent to light up the world
No jewels in glittering hoard?

For, oh my friend, you are wrong, you are wrong,
Your treasures are pearls beyond price.
They may not be Euros or Dollars or Yen,
But those which you have, will suffice.

A helping hand where the path is rough,
A shoulder to mop up the tears.
A friendship that came fair or foul
Stays steadfast through the years.

A kindly word to heal a hurt,
A smile to colour the day.
The warmth of a hug ‘midst arctic wastes,
Kneeling to bless and to pray.

So never say you have nothing to give
Or feel yourself standing apart,
For the world is in need of the healing which comes
From the depths of a generous heart.

Going With The Flow

For every plus, there has to be a minus.
And every minus, likewise, have a plus.
For that’s how everything is kept in balance
Without a lot of argument and fuss.

For every upward swing, there is a downside.
For every sunny smile, there is a frown,
And as some sage once said, so very wisely…
Whatever rises up, must then come down.

If we embrace what Fortune heaps upon us,
Within a thankful blessing, then let go,
We’ll surely hear the rhythm of the cosmos
And harmonise and dance and grow.

Footsteps…

My footsteps left impressions in the snow
Marking out a chanced, haphazard route.
And I could only hope my feet had not
Crushed some hidden, tender, hopeful shoot.

'Twas then I thought to look back down the years
Filled with joy and sorrow, work and play.
And saw the road as smooth as sea-washed sand,
With only fleeting Time to mark the way.

Remembering my rushing heedless haste,
Head in the clouds, awhirl with plan and scheme,
I think of all the lives my path has crossed…
And pray I did not trample on a dream.

Rainbow

We cannot know, my love, I fear
What lies ahead… a smile… a tear,
Despair or hope or joy or woe
Or Life or Death. We cannot know
How straight the path we'll tread together
This year, next year, sometime, never.

So let us pause. Come, take my hand,
For I must make you understand
How very dear you are to me.
You woke my mind and set it free.
You held my heart, a stone cold thing,
And gave it warmth and made it sing.

You coaxed the sunbeams out to play
And chased my shadows clean away.
You turned my darkness into light
And lit the moon and stars at night.
You took the pieces… made a whole
And put a rainbow in my soul.

The Ship

One day, in May, I went to play
As oft I'd done before
Upon the grassy cliff tops,
Which overlook the shore.
I flopped upon my belly
And squinted out to sea
And waited for a pirate ship
To show itself to me.
Her crew, they would be cut-throats,
Their Captain, Fearsome Fred.
He wore a stripey jumper
And a scarf around his head.
Or p'raps there would be smugglers
In little fishing shacks
With kegs of moonshine whiskey
Under piles of rope and sacks.
I scanned the whole horizon
To see what I could spy,
For nothing ever could escape
My telescopic eye.

A scooty clouds played hide and seek
A shaft of brilliant light
Lit up the sea and, "Oh!" I whooped
And shouted with delight.
For there, right there, before me
So wondrous to behold
There sailed a ship, a treasure ship,
All made of burnished gold.
And from her ruby funnels
Billowed rosy, pearly smoke
Which spread around her
Like a lovely, swansdown cloak.
With portholes made of diamonds
And deck of silver gilt
She surely was the fairest
Sailing vessel ever built.
But then the clouds resumed their game
And shuttered out the sun.
My golden ship, she disappeared –
Her hour of glory done.

Instead, a weary steamer
With rusty prow and hull
Went about her daily run,
Her paint all scratched and dull.
And I was filled with wonder
As I thought of all I'd seen.
I knew it was a miracle
Which never might have been.
For if the sun had not shone out
That very moment when
The rusty ship was chugging by
To catch the light, and then

If I had not been there to see
The marvel of it all…
The moment would have passed, and never
Held me in its thrall.
I've locked the memory in my heart
Inside a secret den,
For when I'm grown, I know that I
May need it now and then.

When days are dark, I'll light them with
That play-day by the sea
And reminisce the sun, the ship,
The miracle, and me.

Christine Hornby

Christine Hornby lives in Chorley, Lancashire. She is inspired to write poetry. Throughout her life she has been misunderstood and has had to struggle to communicate with others.

During a bleak period in her life she met her Guardian Angel, who has since guided her on her spiritual path. Today, Christine lives with hope and inner peace.

Through her writing, she has been able to release tension and bring about a balance of wisdom and forgiveness. She has learned that only when you can forgive yourself and surrender your conflicts to God, healing begins. Christine's poetry has truly been 'written out of necessity'; her poems served as an outward expression of her inner pain at a time in her life when she had few to turn to, and while being simple in its style, her poetry could well offer a space in which others could turn to for healing.

Christine is forever mindful that we should be careful of our thoughts, love peacefully and follow our hearts.

Fair

Do you ever feel trapped in a snare?
Do you ever feel nobody is aware?
I have to surrender all this negative consumption -
It is stifling my happiness …a volcanic eruption…
To deny happiness and make sense of people's morals
Leaves an emptiness like an uncrowned royal.

Nobody wishes ill harm to another.
It is 'past hurts' and holding on to sorrow
That causes chaos and confusion.
Only in understanding oneself can clarity shine…
To have wisdom and use it wisely can balance the dance.

Peaceful wishes heal bitterness…
So much to learn in forgiveness, we progress.
Life is fair and people care…
It is full of colour lighting up the air.

The senses sublimely capturing a beautiful aroma,
The birds singing in the distance…chanting hills.
The waterfalls spectacularly thundering down mountains,
Whilst farmers nurture and attune their flock.

The trees gigantic and richly majestic,
The animals' free spirits neither captive nor domestic.
The land filled with unimaginable colours
The day gives pleasure to more than a few.
The towns are lit by welcoming sights.
From coast to coast the lighthouse glows.

In some parts of the world sun and moon take precedence
Complete darkness falling within an eclipse.
So many sensations and life experiences
Give awareness to souls, enriched.

My life is fair. I am fortunate, I know -
I searched for God so often, I was never alone.
I begged and pleaded to have help for others
But must start with helping myself. Now I shudder.
It took me many years of being a coward and feeling scared,
My mind was determined to be positive and to share.
I haven't changed too much, I like to smile and care.
I endeavour to savour all that life offers, now aware.
I will take stock and not compromise the lot,
By appreciating that circumstances gave me a rod.
To be open with self and honest with my feelings
Now my new world is fruitful and pleasing
Never again have doubts in the universe
God speaks to us verse after verse.

Middle of the Garden

In the middle of the garden
I smell beautiful fragranced roses;
Red, yellow orange and white.
Golden haze through the trees from sunlight,
There is an arch made of ancient oak -
Once an energised tree, just needed nurturing from folk.
The tree gave so much pleasure -
Like a resting place for buried treasure
The middle of the garden, my place
A place where my heartbeat steadily paced.

Breathing in, out in a calm manner
Aware of serenity, Lord of the Manor.
My place is simply a haven to me
Memories of past, in awareness I see
Living in the now, blessed with spirituality,
Contemplating on the future, guided along
The middle of the garden is where I belong,
Living each day, asking for help to be strong,
Trying to do good deeds to compensate for wrongs.
Encouraged by the tunes of the birds' hopeful songs
My life is richer than I could have imagined,
Learning and growing with positive actions
Trying my best on the earth to be wise.
I am challenged and feel have a purpose in life
In the middle of the garden sensing solitude.
I am a colourful person - I got rid of my blues,
Enjoy offering upliftment and comforting news.
Blessed with magical moments, spiritually open
The middle of the garden where love is spoken.

Listen

I can hear
My jaw was clicking
The bird fluttered its wings
The cage sounded loud
Traffic roared like thunder
The motorway sounded like rockets launching
What a lot of noises, I could hear
The clock is ticking, tick, tick and tick
So loud, it sounds like an angry knock
The bird singing spontaneously

Its claws clatter round the cage
Still aware of my breathing
I am relaxed and listening
The television makes a sound
My thoughts are drifting
My energy is on previous conversation
Stop, listen, and train your ears
It is relaxing, everything becomes clear
Creaking floor boards, then a bump
More creaking, no I am not drunk
Next door bang their door
And another neighbour's barking dog
Now the only sound tick, tick and tick
Not for long barking dogs
Not much silence in using ears
I prefer to meditate or have a glass of beer
In listening with my ears
There is nothing to fear
But it was my choice
To listen to all that noise.

Society

Society has it all worked out -
They think they know what life is all about.
Some get angry and scream and shout;
Others suffer in silence and do not let anger out.
People come from all over the world
And some are attacked, abuse is hurled.
Their skin may be different, sometimes burned,
They suffer from cruelty, sometimes pitied,

They may be rich and have lots of wealth,
Some have very little and in ill health.
Babies are born and brought up with care;
Some have no idea who they are,
But there are those who are well aware
Of the abundance of love with a look (not a stare)
That children learn from their parents.
Not all parents get it right with common sense -
Some are strict and build a fence
To protect their children in their defence.
Teenagers grow and, with learning,
Seek to be themselves and enjoying
They sometimes rebel from all their upbringing
And others rejoice in their growing and changing.
Adults are often portrayed as being strong
Some get their lives and perception all wrong.
There are those with a positive outlook,
Those who are humble and calm with a look,
There are old and young in the universe.
Good, bad, sweetness and bitterness…
Those who have learned their journey have bliss
When society makes no judgement;
Their thoughts are purest.
In love and in loving we are blessed;
A peaceful society will work out.

Never

You never understand me
You never knew my world
Why, oh why could you not see?
You gave me possessions
They meant more to you, not me.
Gentle arms with compassion
Feeling encompassed with serenity.

It was my desperate need
For you to love me -
You said it many times -
But you did not read the signs;
I was in denial and frightened.

My head was full of confusion;
Lies and toxic infusion.
I met many complicated souls;
Their lives were also dingy black holes,
All I wanted to feel was love.

I almost died before I realised
God has love and gives it no matter
Even if I am viewed up as a *mad hatter*.
I communicate and understand,
I experienced similar,
But now my life is clearer.

I am mature and have learned lessons,
And my understanding for another
Is within my knowledge.

When I started to understand me
I became aware and full of glee.

It took me a lifetime
Before I was nourished and felt
Love for me,
But it was worth all that pain
Because now I receive love
Like a black cloud gives rain.
I am complicated no more
And with love my soul grows.

I try to do my best -
I am not perfect, just human like the rest.
I never try to judge people,
I never doubt that I am loved.
Thank you for never ever doubting me -
I learned about love the hard way
But love is my strength day after day.

I Love Myself!

"I love myself!"
"Sorry,
Say that again."
"I love myself."
"I can't believe you said that.
How long has it been?"
"So long I can't remember…
I have never respected me."

I let others control and prosecute me
I took all that nonsense.
I let others see I was worthless,
I had no thought for me.
I cared so much for others
And never realised that the problems
Were programmed inside me -
I thought it was selfish to look after me.
But was a concept, I had to change.
Without my health
There is no chance of wealth.
Without an open heart filled with love
I cannot raise myself to be compassionate,
But now I know that I have love -
The one who cares and has love for me.
Loving me is compassion, too,
And maybe I have just helped you

Patience

I have never been patient
I have never been tolerant
I have been judgemental -
Hell, I have been a bad patient!

But I have learned to accept
We need to be calm and kind,
Not rude and harmful to all mankind.
This is when we grow and correct
All the nonsense that we have caused
Because we were so impatient.

But being kind to ourselves
Is the least best possible solution.

Now I am learning to love
And put all the hurt behind -
Truly I am gaining wisdom.
I pray someday that
I will have lots of patience
And walk tall, with contentment,
Knowing I am patient.

Courage

That is all it takes
Courage to make
Your come awake
Courage to stand tall
Then you never look small
Courage to say, "No"
Courage to sow a new seed
You know
Courage to listen
To your inner voice
This is in silence
Not with lots of noise
Courage to believe
That you have made
A selfless choice, not to be afraid
Courage to see the truth
With wisdom and peace
Courage can solve your greatest needs
Much awareness is clear

When you have courage to steer
Yourself and your conscience
Not accepting other people's nonsense
Courage to follow yourself
And know you are respectful
Courage to remain positive and helpful
Courage to be who you really are
And that is a wonderful shining star
Then there is a vibrant light shining from you
It is with courage that one can establish
The difference in friendship
And mindful tricks
A friend will always leave you smiling
Never left hurt or crying
But with courage
Rage not with anger
But grow with love stronger and stronger
With love from your heart
And courage to stay apart
From persuasion to be swayed
Just because all others follow
Sometimes leaves you numb and hollow
But with courage you will see
It takes courage
To believe in you and me.

I Am Happy

I am happy.
What makes you happy?
A smile on someone's face,
My eyes seeing so much joy
I now run my own race.
If I smile, it is through love
Because it comes from above.

I am happy
I am alive
I can breathe the air
And feel free to care.
My hair blows gently in the breeze
I can walk miles, in silence please.
The thoughts are pleasant, of mountain air,
The waterfalls tumble, in amazement, I stare.
The scenic route filled with green
Healing all the energies resources -
Nature so beautiful - I have seen
The trees soar high to reach the sky
The day is so many colours and night
No night for batteries and torches
The sun and moon take care of the light
What a wondrous sight
How could I not be happy?

I sensed the calm of the sea
How striking was the vast ocean
I saw the colour turquoise
Deep blue, greens and currents changing
With the captain and crew safely navigating.

I am so happy to be alive
And appreciate all the beauty I can see
How could I not be happy?
I just need love and inner peace to survive.

I am happy
I have grown so much
I am no longer out of touch
I am thankful, I have many friends…
Not those who drive me round the bend,
But those who care and positively share.
Upliftment, kindness and loving meaning to an end…
It is the healing angels God sends.

I am happy.
It is in silence that I learn
To empty my mind and stop yearning
Because I have stopped searching -
I have found who I am.
I am happy, content,
Not negative for a moment -
Over my head with silly comments!
No more fears - endless fears -
I haven't been this happy in years.

Alone

I am watching a leaf
Blowing on the end of the branch.
The branch is bare but for this leaf
The branch is part of an enormous tree.

The wind blows hard,
The leaf is discoloured -
It is winter you see.
The rain falls down
The leaf touches the ground.

Will the leaf make compost?
Or travel to another coast -
It could make a home
Or be shredded and torn.

A new life for this tree…
Part of a bigger tree,
But one thing for certain
It will be part of the next generation.

With love and care for our nation
We can see beauty in God's creation.
A single leaf
A big oak tree
So much life
Without a fight.

So much awareness
Life as a meaning
See beauty in everything
A single leaf surviving
So much joy in living
Take joy in receiving
As well as giving.

Angry At The World

I think I was born angry
I have always been angry at the world
I do not know how I survived.
I think boxing gloves and a punch bag
Would have shredded those knotted rags
I have always been angry at the world.

People would see me smile
And once in a while I would drop my barrier
But this did not work in my favour
I was often ridiculed for my behaviour.
I learned valuable lessons
When I beat myself in rage of heat
My soul and body are a precious gift
I am no more in resentful rift.

I am anger-free and have seen the monster within
I did not see before, but there are poorer than me.
My eyes are open, I am aware
The lessons learned, I really do care.
My body need nourishment and to be loved by me
My soul will glow and the world will know
With God's help and compassion
I am angry no more.

Rug Pulled

When the rug has been pulled from beneath you
And you feel your dreams lost too
A blanket of warmth will enfold you
And another destiny follows through.

The past gives life experiences
The future peace and happiness
It is harmful to hold on to bitterness
Nothing is gained in being too serious.

Instead, breathe out with a deep sigh
Stand tall and hold your head up high
Because a wise soul knows
Where peace and laughter grows
A magical journey unfolds.

There is a bright future out there
Just waiting for you to make that step
It's exciting and rewarding,
Like having a second chance.
It takes a transformation
To battle through and show the nation
"I'm not down for long when I'm guided by my Angels."

Communication

It is not hard to say,
"I do not understand."
It is not hard to say,
"Can I help you?"
To be able to communicate
Is the essence of understanding.
Learning comes from compassion,
Compassion comes from the heart.
When the heart is open
True words are spoken
But compassion sometimes hurts,
Because we do not like
To think of ourselves as cruel.
We may not realise
We are hurting anyone -
Actions speak volumes.
Some actions add fore to the fuel,
We don't always see the picture -
Our path is our learning,
Wisdom comes when communicating.
Communication is only possible when listening.
In listening we can hear every sound…
Resonating from our feelings.
In communicating we can sense
How another person is feeling.
We can communicate with kindness.
I love the sweetness
We can communicate with empathy,
"I am here for you whenever you need me."
We can communicate anger…
I hate people who talk down to others.

We can communicate our feelings
By touch, facial expression and verbally;
We let others know how we feel
By walking and dragging our heels,
By drooping our head and shoulders,
By shouting, screaming and feeling mad,
But not by stepping back, lost and sad.
Through the tears rolling uncontrollably down our cheeks
Not expecting this moment to cease.
By smiling and laughing we help others release
All the tensions inside if they fall down to their knees.
By communicating we have a bigger picture;
No one ought be selfish, we have so much to endure;
When we talk openly to another
We can share our experiences clear the air.
For some in need of a little friendship
Communication can resolve broken relationships;
Just by writing a letter or picking up the phone
May help a person to decide to come home.
People can change and have a transformation -
Being able to communicate is a real salvation -
It gives an understanding of people's beliefs
When judging others look at yourself please
Every time we communicate
Let us smile with joy
Knowing that we spoke wisely,
Just a pleasant encounter
Giving support to a lonely person
Help them to become strong.
Humility comes from souls alike
Who do not pretend to like you.
It is obvious with the look in their eyes
They do not look down at you
Because everyone is equal and unique.

When communication is expressed
With good intentions
We can all make a difference.
God is wisdom, love and compassion
Communicating through his angels and guides.
God is helping us to strive
To live peacefully with our life.

Adventure

We all have a sense of adventure
It is a challenge deep inside.
We push all boundaries -
Feel accomplished with pride.
Never looking at danger, nor tense with fear
Taking steps into the unknown.
Never alone, a new you is born.
Having a sense of adventure
Neither fear nor feeling numbness,
Encompasses you with abundance.
Restoring a balance and taking a chance -
Have courage to face life and hopefulness -
Bless every new beginning with thankfulness,
Having a sense of adventure
Can bring spiritual enlightenment.
You can learn skills you never imagined -
Believing and trusting can lead to joy never ending.
It takes strength and wishful intent,
Exciting new dreams are heaven sent,
Accept love and nurturing
Enjoy life adventuring
To have a sense of adventure you must venture.

Birds

Birds singing
So much peace and love.
To soar high like the golden eagle
In stillness
Watching the wings spread wide
Gives so much joy -
Makes me want to fly
Another dimension in the sky.
Other species can:
The bat is a mammal with wings
Bats circle around the moon.
I must try to give love to all -
Bats deserve love and nurturing too
Not just a certain few…
The ugly duckling
Spring to mind.
I have felt lonely;
Birds are similar to me and you -
They survive and try to live socially.
Some die because of their beauty,
Others die in captivity.
Birds love to be free -
They can live in open space,
Can travel at speed and race.
I thank God for birds when I pray -
Birds really do brighten my day -
Restore good thoughts in my mind.
So much upliftment,
Birds singing.

Mind

Mind you don't fall
Mind you don't slip
Mind you listen when we call
Mind you have a good trip
Mind over matter
Mind can overcome disaster
Mindfulness in how you speak
Mindfulness in how you teach

Mindfulness in respecting one another
Mindfulness in loving our sisters and brothers
Mind your thoughts
Mind you live in the now
Mind you give good responses
Mind you thank your lucky stars
Mind you appreciate who you are!
Mind you take good care
Mind you always be aware

Mind you look after yourself
Mindfulness in loving self
Mind to make choices
Mindfulness in choosing noises
Mind you grow tall
Mindfulness in being small
Mind can be a learning master
Mindfulness in greener pastures

Mind given to all mankind
Mind unique and vastly chimed
Mindfulness in knowing your goal
Mind you love every heart and soul
Mind and rejoice and thank our Lord
Mind you try to do good deeds
Mindfulness in sowing new seeds
Mind you learn when you fall
Mindfulness in wisdom
In our beautiful inheritance

Mind you accept the mind is complex
Mind you grow wise from every test
Mind you always give your best
Mindfulness in what you seek
Mind what company you keep
Mind you are always grounded
Mindfulness is wonderfully astounding
Mind is enriched when no longer doubting
Mindfulness is life's circle never ending

Ladder

I lost my rung on the ladder
I lost everything, I was afraid.
Fear took over me
I had to be stronger
My sadness was lifted
The bad days gone
I found one step on the ladder
Now I am holding on.

The times ahead
Were challenges of dread.
My smile, genuine,
I had happy thoughts in my head,
I had captured something pure.
God only knows what pressure
Took my soul from grandeur -
It was love and nurturing.
My head submerged in a good book -
So much to gain by breathing…
Every breath reinforcing vitality.
Discovering life, as with many visionaries,
Hopeful to reinforce visibility
To those who neglect responsibilities.
It gave me the meaning of a glorious life force.
Only in contemplating I saw much more
It is our steps lighting up the way for others.
When we stop destroying man,
Women, animals and our nature land,
Then we live in harmony and appreciate birth.
A rung on the ladder gave me a new worth,
Not to take anything for granted and live happy.
We can all regret past events but reality
Comes to us all in tranquillity and inner strength,
Not sacrificing love given.
Rejoicing and thanking every breath taken,
God gives us a ladder whenever
We reach for his hand;
Each time a new rung on the ladder
Reaching to the gates of Heaven.
I am thankful for all that I have been given…
Whatever life offers there is always a ladder
We can accept our life and look at the good,

Rather than withering, death or simply giving up -
We can inspire others by climbing up.
God is in charge and never leaves us;
We are all his children, in his likeness,
And we are granted his forgiveness, whatever our foolishness.
God grants us wisdom, love and peace -
Only a thought away when we seek.
In praying for lost souls
The rung on the ladder is complete.

Surrender

Can I surrender all my fears to you?
Can I be open and honest with you?
I feel stupendous warmth and calm
To be able to express myself without harm.
Yes, I can surrender my fears to you.

Can I surrender my enemies to you?
They misunderstood me and saw me as weak.
I feel with understanding my self I shine -
My shoulders droop no more
Content, I stand refined.
Yes, I can surrender my enemies to you.

Can I surrender my worries to you?
My worries are my doing, caused by guilt and pain.
My heart beats heavily if I suffer in vain,
I need to detach from unconquerable fate.
My heart beats rhythmically, feeling safe -
Yes, I can surrender my worries to you.

Can I surrender my ego to you?
Sometimes I hurt people and become selfish -
I forget who is in charge and follow the wrong band
I have a choice, but my heart beats with your command.
Yes, I can surrender my ego to you

Can I surrender my tears to you?
I have cried so hard I feared I would not stop.
By my own actions I weep in intertwining knots;
I am fortunately aware that you dry my tears.
Yes, I can surrender my tears to you.

You give me strength to help me live courageously.
My actions are my choosing, whether right or wrong,
Yes, I can surrender - my loving heart is now strong.
God never lets us down, his love is magnified -
Surrender your feelings to God and his love is intensified.
Yes, I can surrender my feelings. God always be my guide.

Million

A million grains of sand
A million outstretched hands
Many lost souls holding on
Hoping someone to their aid will come
So many people wishing their lives were full
So many people not knowing how to have fun
A million chances to win the lottery
A million steps to reach solitary

A million questions asked daily
A million reasons given effortlessly
Only by questioning oneself
Can one gain answers within
Like soul searching and asking why
There are injustices and cruel atrocities

A million prayers offered for peace
A million contradictions to harmony
One can only start with peaceful thoughts
The love sent to another will transmute
Like the angels playing the violin and flute
God has the answers in love not war
We need to express our feelings more

A million carers looking out for the suffering
A million professionals teaching their students
So much to be gained from respecting our elders
They are our teachers and become our masters
The masters have learned through many lessons
The lessons have been hard earned and mastered
Not to do harm when someone has hurt you
But pray for that person it could be you

A million drops of water make an ocean
A million particles of matter pollute the air
We can all make a difference in love and prayer
In thanking God for every single moment
In respecting every part of our existence
We can grow in harmony with one another
By sharing not moaning but happy in knowing
That we are blessed a million ways

A million soldiers go to war
A million soldiers kill a million more
What is the sense of armies destroying one another?
Families are torn on either side
Someone has lost a father or brother
Could be a sister or a mother
No sense when peace can restore harmony and love
A million ways to communicate with another.

A million ways to abuse someone
It could be by using words or attacking with intent
Think carefully what you say and the aggression
It can leave the person a wreck and terribly confused
Please treat others like you like to be treated yourself
Be kind and gentle and do not worry about mistakes
Mistakes help you to grow and benefit your soul

A million ways to be kind to someone
Smile and offer them a kind word
Do not be aggressive towards them
Instead accept them for who they are
Do not wish harmful attacks on their families
Wish them love, harmony and peace
If they are hungry, share your food with them
A million ways to make a difference
Start now by changing your mind, be kind.

A million different points of view
I have just given a few
Many have different agendas
But with greed there is no satisfaction
Because it does nor resolve corruption
In having enough and giving to the poor
Can result in a million have a new transformation?
A million ways to help those less fortunate, feel radiant
A million lost souls not deprived by given a new lease of life.

Ann F. Bell

Ann lives in Wickford, Essex with her husband John and their pets. She derives a lot of love from her pets especially as she suffers from ME. This has not stopped her from writing poetry, however, or from studying History of Art and History through the Open University.
She is developing her skills as a spiritual medium and would one day like to run her own development circle. Ann also keeps busy as a member of a Book Group and a member of the Sherlock Holmes Society.
In appreciation of the support (both earthly and spiritual) of her family and friends, including her parents and Aunt K, Ann has dedicated this collection to them.

A Bed of Green

A bed of green
We once lay upon.
The stars were shining;
The sun still shone.

A bed of blue
Then came my way.
I begged you, “Please
Don’t go away.”

Now upon a bed of white,
I know I leave
The world tonight.

I’ve felt the blue
And loved the green;
But most of all
Been touched by you.

A Spirit Appears Before me

A spirit appears before me -
Look inside your book.
"Why?" I said, asking.
"Believe," it said,
"Just look."

A feather of the purest white,
Untouched like gentle snow,
From an angels wing
You ask, "How do you know?"

The spirit was my daughter
Who left us long ago.
The tears we weep must hurt them
As our grief, likes a river's flow.

"Don't cry anymore," she told me,
"I'm with you for all time,
Taking care of the ones I love…
Being united in time to come."

Changes

He's coming now -
The Stranger,
His footsteps on the stair.
My husband, now a stranger,
Is standing sadly there.

Dedicated to a Patient I Nursed who Sadly Died

I feel so lonely sitting here -
Alone in this wheelchair.
It seems that everyone passing by
Just turns with a knowing stare.

Do they know I can't live without love,
Or of the pain that gets harder to bear
As I cry out for compassion…
A hand that says, "I care?"

I dream of my love that is now lost
In the deep passages of time,
And feel this disease that cripples me
Is their sentence to my crime.

What sin have I committed?
Being in love was my only crime…
To cry out when they turn away
From a man who's run out of time.

Of the love I bore and that bore me
I do not regret one day,
But how I wish the end would come
For this pain be taken away

Do Not Grieve When I am Gone

Do not grieve when I am gone -
My love my poetry will live on.
It shows my emotions, declares my love -
For all of nature, the stars above

Do not cry when I am gone
My soul lives on in a blackbird's song
In the smile of a child, in her sweet tears;
I leave my strength so know no fear.

But most of all I leave you joy
To share with man, woman or boy
A smile that lights a young girl's face;
The delight that is felt in a first embrace.

From baby to ageing I send you health
A gift that is greater than fame or wealth
Each day to bring no grief, no fears,
But love and comfort throughout the years.

Dreading the Night

Dreading the night
He walks alone
To find his love
And bring her home.

I did her wrong,
Now I must pay -
If they cared at all
They'd go away.

We came to see if it is true
That some who die don't rest;
To hear from you we hope
To put our theory to the test.

That we are right
And they are wrong,
No pity have we
For your plaintive song.

A lady came into the room,
"Leave him alone," she sighed,
"We just want to help him."
How indignantly they lied.

She turned and said,
"Don't stay here,
I will show the way."
He entered the light
That wonderful day.

Dreaming

Sunshine glints on whitewash stone,
While sunspots dapple and gleam.
A soft sweet breeze blows gently
And ripples the silent stream.

An idyllic picture of country grace.
A young man looks on the scene,
He seems bewitched by the view
But it plays out its life unseen.

How sad he was to lie there
With beauty all around,
Listening for steps he longs to hear
But comes no sight nor sound.

Their dream of love has faded,
Many forces drove them apart.
She could not wed without consent
So he lies with broken heart.

Not wishing to see with open eyes,
He must go his lonely way.
A dreamer, a thinker, a poet -
He will look to happier days.

Emily Jane

An Angel's breath just kissed my cheek -
It's a taste so sweet and pure.
I stand bewitched by soft beauty
And the power of strange allure.

This Angel has no wings to fly
It's a spirit earthly bound -
A voice so soft that calls to me
With tone of musical sound.

This Angel child has touched my heart
With innocent trusting ways -
Tiny hand clutched tight to mine
I am humbled by her gaze.

Hello up There

Hello up there
It's me down here
You're so tall
And I'm so small
But we are equal aren't we?

His Strong Arms Shield me Like Wool

His strong arms shield me like wool,
His gentle words heal my pain,
His breath on my hair gentle as angels,
Sweet kisses reveal his love.

When young his arms held me tightly,
His words of love captured my heart,
His breath on my hair hot with desire,
With kisses revealing his love.

I Saw From the Corner of my Eye

I saw from the corner of my eye
A tiny fly come sailing by.
"Well," I said, "Your time is near."
"How will you do this?" he asked with fear.

"With a newspaper swatter," I said with a grin.
"I wouldn't advise it if you knew where I'd been.
Look up above," he said with a smile,
As hundreds of flies seemed to spread for miles.
I conceded this time and sat with a bow;
I shall put my paper away for now.
"When you're alone one day little friend,
Look out, for I mean that to be your end."

We battled on for many years
But like most things it ends in tears -
Not for the fly, who flew away,
But my leg I broke that fatal day.
I jumped on a stool
And said with a thrill,
"I've got you now!"
I saw him shiver with a chill
Then he smiled. "What's that about?"
I thought to myself, and with a shout
Tottered and fell onto the floor.
With shaking hand I tell you more -
Landing badly on one leg,
I felt it shatter like an egg.
Now he sits and talks to me
We share a biscuit and sweet tea.

My Father

Where are you now my long lost friend
As I journey this road of pain?
You who kept me from harm;
My heart aches for you again.

For a love so selfless given
To a child so full of fear,
Of oncoming years no knowledge within,
Protecting, guiding the age of growing.

As you now so softly sleep
In your cold and lonely grave,
I feel your love and guidance
Reach out to keep me safe.

Not to be

The moon sees me as I sit alone
Contemplating the end of life,
When love was new and full of hope…
Soon to be a wife.

Fate prophesied a different way,
Your love was just a lie.
Sitting here she watches still
Like her to wane and die.

Reflections on Trains

I see the many faces,
Some looking sad and drawn -
Others on their way to dream
What happens at break of dawn.

Some will wake with lovers
As yet who have no name -
Others will lie awake and sigh
At love's sweet fragile frame.

They work, they talk, they dream
Of future plans ahead,
And wait again until the dawn
When sleeping thoughts are shed.

Reverie

Gently, sweetly, breathing deeply,
My baby soft and new.
Angels watch until the morning -
My life I dedicate to you.

It's many years now and you've grown
And taken yourself a wife.
Still my angels, watch and guide
My love, my sweet, my life.

Secret Thoughts

I need you now
So please don't shout,
I'm drowning in my thoughts.
Unable to grasp what's happening -
How lonely and wanting
To be held with love -
How I wish you wouldn't shout.

I'm shouting again
But wish I wouldn't,
Unable to grasp what's happening
You're sitting huddled with hidden expression.
How lonely I feel, perhaps I hate you now.
Stop looking at me with those beautiful eyes.
Looking now realising I love you -
How I wish I wouldn't shout.

Should I Have Tried to Make Him Stay?

Should I have tried to make him stay?
How he loved with such selfless thought;
He clothed my soul with words of love
How could I say the words
He longed to hear?

My mind caught in a timeless warp,
Forever bound with secret thought;
For I couldn't give this man my heart,
Being broken by love
Years before.

The Man in the White Shirt Lay Dying

The man in the white shirt lay dying
Dying … his blood all around,
While the robotic arm continued
Stabbing, without a sound.

"Please stop," he whispered, lips as cold as ice.
With grieving heart the robot replied,
"You've dared to question our Master,
This comes at a terrible price.

Not just for you but mankind"
"Your voice made so much sense;
In my own way I'm dying - duty my only defence."

With him died all reason;
The Man of the Word had won.
"Take him away, this traitor,
And dispose of him my son."

The boy had dared to question
The Lord of all the Words.
"The Law, my Word, is final."
No cry of sorrow could be heard.

The man of the Word was lonely -
All love for him had died.
He issued a warning decree;
Still he refused to see.

"I demand that you all love me -
My word is the law of reason."
Then in his waking dreams the sight
Of the broken young man in white.

"I killed this child for daring,
To oppose my reason," he cried,
But his robotic arm remembered
That the age of reason had died.

Thoughts

Down, down into
The dark abyss of time,
Sinking lower in to the
Void inside my mind,
I long to make sense of life
And its reason,
But emptiness is all I find.

Watching Sleeping

Watching, sleeping,
Hearing the breathing -
I want him.

Seeing him waking
In dawn's grey light -
I reach for him.

Watching his eyes,
Caressing my need -
I feel him.

When loving is over,
Content once more -
I love him.

When Will it Happen?

When will it happen?
When will I know
If the whole of my life
Is to stay or to go?

For so many years
We've lived as one,
But a stranger between us
And you will soon be gone.

This emotion you're feeling -
Is it love, or just fear?
The last chance you're given,
When afraid of the coming years.

Your new love is younger,
Far much younger than I.
I fear for your soul
Seeing through your lies.

I'm waiting now, how still the night.
Will you answer … "Will it be me?"
I hear you crying, your silent touch.
Can you tell me what it's to be?

When will it happen?
Will I now cry?
In my arms now, you're saying
You've told your love, "Goodbye."

This book is dedicated to anyone who
has used poetry as a vehicle for self-
expression and self-healing.
If it feels necessary to be written,
then it ought to be!

Published by Spiritual Path Books UK
ISBN 978-0-9558832-3-1

Tel: 07887 500125
spiritualpath@yahoo.co.uk